# HORSES

# ARABIAN HORSES

# JANET L. GAMMIE

## ABDO & Daughters

Published by Abdo & Daughters, 4940 Viking Drive, Suite 622, Edina, Minnesota 55435.´

Library bound edition distributed by Rockbottom Books, Pentagon Tower, P.O. Box 36036, Minneapolis, Minnesota 55435.

Printed in the United States.

Cover Photo credit: Peter Arnold, Inc.
Interior Photo credits: Peter Arnold, Inc. pages 5, 7, 11, 17, 19

Julie Green, pages 9, 13, 21

**Edited by Bob Italia**

**Library of Congress Cataloging-in-Publication Data**

Gammie, Janet L.
    Arabian Horses/ Janet L. Gammie.
        p.   cm. — (Horses)
    Includes bibllographical references (p.23) and index.
        ISBN 1-56239-440-1
    1. Arabian horse—Juvenile literature [. Arabian horse. 2. Horses.] I. Title. II. Series:
Gammle, Janet L. Horses.
SF293.A8G36    1995
636.1'12—dc20

95-3369
CIP
AC

**ABOUT THE AUTHOR**
    Janet Gammie has worked with thoroughbred race horses for over 10 years. She trained and galloped thoroughbred race horses while working on the racetracks and farms in Louisiana and Arkansas. She is a graduate of Louisiana Tech University's Animal Science program with an equine specialty.

# Contents

# WHERE ARABIANS CAME FROM

Horses are mammals just like humans. Mammals are warm-blooded animals with a backbone. Their body heat comes from inside their body.

The horses earliest **ancestor** was *Eohippus* (e-oh-HIP-us). It lived about 50 million years ago and was 12 inches (30 cm) high. The oldest known **domesticated** horse is said to be the Persian Arabian.

Arabian horses first appeared on the Arabian Peninsula over 2,000 years ago.

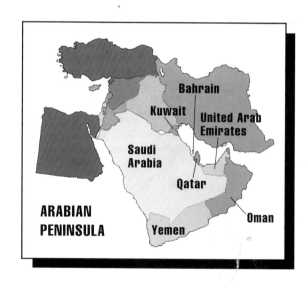

4

**The Arabian horse.**

An Arabian horse appeared on the first known statue of a horse and rider.

There are three different types of horses: hot bloods, cold bloods and warm bloods. These terms refer to their birth place and not their body temperature. Arabians are hot bloods. They first appeared on the **Arabian Peninsula** over 2,000 years ago.

# WHAT ARABIANS LOOK LIKE

The Arabian has a sleek head, broad forehead and narrow **muzzle** with a dip in the middle. The eyes are large and set far apart. They have long, wide necks. Their long silky **manes** and tails are set high on their short backs. Some Arabians have one less rib than other horse **breeds**.

Arabians stand 14 to 15 hands high (hh). Each hand equals 4 inches (10 cm). They weigh 800 to 1,000 pounds (363 to 454 kilograms).

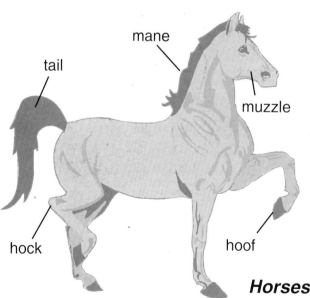

mane

tail

muzzle

hock

hoof

*Horses share the same features.*

**Purebred** Arabians can be any solid color. Purebred means the horse is not mixed with any other horse breed.

*The Arabian has a sleek head, broad forehead and large eyes that are set far apart.*

# WHAT MAKES ARABIANS SPECIAL

For thousands of years, the Arabian has been **bred** for its speed and strength. The desert tribesmen of the **Middle East** needed horses that could live in hot and cold temperatures with little food or water. Today, Arabians compete in many sports including racing, showing, driving and long-distance riding.

No other breed equals the Arabian at long-distance events. Many other horse breeds are bred with Arabians to improve their strength. Arabians are the founding **sires** of the **thoroughbred**. Like all hot bloods, they are lively and brave animals.

*Arabian horses compete in many sports including racing, showing, driving, and long-distance riding.*

# COLOR

Breeders prefer solid colored Arabians. Common colors are bay, chestnut, black, roan, or gray. Bay is a light or dark brown body with black points. Points are the horse's legs, **mane** and tail.

A horse with brown hair and the same color or lighter points is a chestnut. Black horses have all black hairs and can have white markings. Markings are a solid white patch of color on the head and legs. The five basic head markings are star, stripe, blaze, snip, and white face. An Arabian can have different mixes of any of these head markings. Leg markings are ankle, sock, and stocking. Arabians can have any mixes of leg markings.

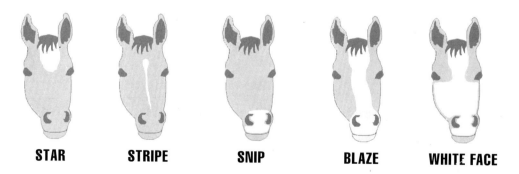

**STAR**　　**STRIPE**　　**SNIP**　　**BLAZE**　　**WHITE FACE**

*Spotted Arabians are often not accepted as a true Arabian breed.*

Roan is one basic color with one or more colors added. Gray horses have white and black hairs on black skin. Gray horses usually turn white with age. Spotted Arabians are often not accepted as a true Arabian **breed**. Bays and grays are the most popular colors.

# CARE

Horses are vaccinated (VAK-sin-ay-ted) regularly to protect them from disease and sickness. A vaccination is a shot. Regular **deworming** keeps the horse free of internal parasites. Daily **grooming** keeps the skin and coat free of external parasites. A parasite is a bug that lives off of another animal. Parasites cause sickness and sometimes death.

The horse's teeth grow throughout its life. They become uneven and sharp with age. When this happens the teeth are "floated" or filed down. Uneven and sharp teeth can cause many health problems.

**Trimming** their hooves helps prevent hoof and leg problems. Hooves are like human fingernails. They continue to grow throughout the horse's life.

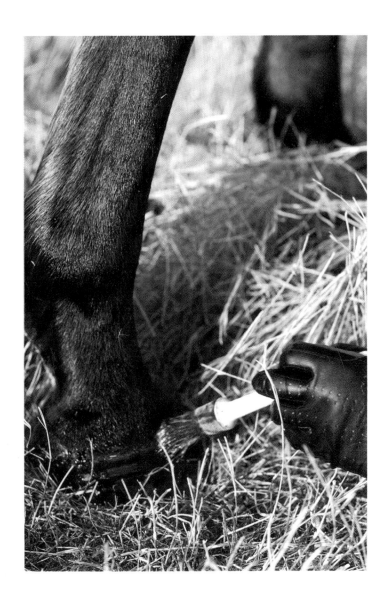

*Arabians should be groomed before and after riding.*

# FEEDING

Horses need food to grow and develop. Hay, grass or alfalfa, grain and water are staples. These staples can be given alone or mixed together. Grains include oats, wheat, barley, and corn. Oats can be mixed with other grains or fed alone. Hays and grains are fed in proper levels to meet a horse's **nutritional** needs.

Nutritional needs depend on age, how much the horse has grown, and type of training. The more work a horse does, the more food it will need for energy. A horse that is not growing or working should need only hay. Horses that are **stabled** will be fed differently than those kept outside. Fresh water should always be given. A horse can survive only a few days without water.

*Arabians need food to grow and develop. Hay, grass, alfalfa, grain and water are very important.*

# THINGS ARABIANS NEED

**Saddles** and **bridles** are the basic equipment needed to ride a horse. There are two types of saddles: the Western saddle and the English saddle. The Western saddle is used for long-distance riding like **herding** cattle. The English saddle is used for trick riding like jumping.

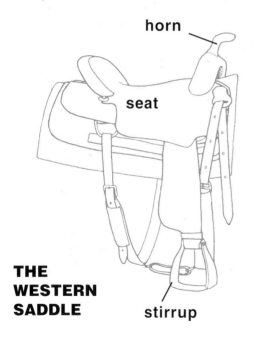

horn

seat

**THE WESTERN SADDLE**

stirrup

The bridle goes over the horse's head. It is used for control. There are three parts to the bridle: the **headstall**, the **bit** and the **reins**. The headstall goes over the horse's ears and around the chin. It attaches to the bit. The bit then attaches to the reins.

All **bridles** have a **headstall** and **reins**.

All bridles do not have a **bit**. There is a bitless bridle called the bosal.

There are many types of brushes used for **grooming** the horse's **coat**. A hoof pick removes dirt and stones from the the horse's hooves.

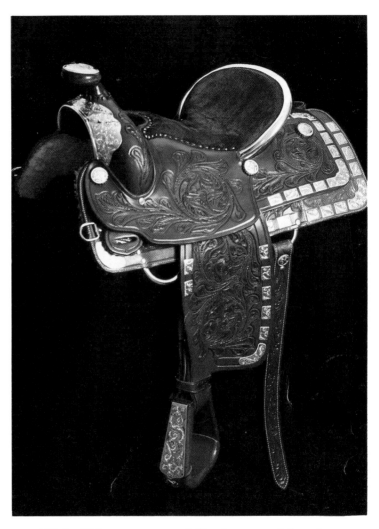

*This Western saddle is used for long-distance riding like herding cattle.*

# HOW ARABIANS GROW

A baby horse is called a foal. A young male horse is called a colt. After he is two years old, he is called a stallion. A young female horse is called a filly. After she is two years old she is called a mare.

A foal lives inside the mare's body for about 11 months. A foal takes its first wobbly steps 15 minutes after birth. In an hour or two a foal will **nurse** and can run. A few days after birth a foal starts to grow teeth. Within a week it can eat grass.

After 3 to 4 months, the foal can live without the mare's milk. Young horses spend their first year playing and growing. During this time the foal learns skills like jumping, running and balance.

*Young Arabians spend their first year playing and growing.*

# TRAINING

Arabians are used in many sports. They are best known for their speed and skill at long-distance riding. They are also used to drive, race and show. Driving means to pull a cart or wagon. In **ancient** times, Arabians pulled **chariots**.

The type of training will depend on the sport for which the horse is used. All horses learn to wear a **halter** a few days after birth. As the foal grows, it will learn to walk beside a person.

In its second year, the Arabian will learn to **lunge** on a lunge line. A lunge line is a long rope on which a horse can walk, **trot**, and **canter** in a large circle. This is called "ground work." The horse will then be **saddled** for the first time. In the horse's third or fourth year, it starts its training for riding, showing or driving.

*In the Arabian's third or fourth year it starts its training for riding, showing or driving.*

# GLOSSARY

**ANCESTOR** (AN-ses-tor) - An animal from which other animals are descended.

**ANCIENT** (AIN-chent) - Very old.

**ARABIAN PENINSULA** - The land mass that includes the Middle East countries of Saudi Arabia, Kuwait, Bahrain, Oman, Yemen, Qatar, and the United Arab Emirates.

**BIT** - The metal piece of a bridle that goes in the horse's mouth.

**BREED** - To produce young; also, a group of animals that look alike and have the same ancestor.

**BRIDLE** - The part of the harness that fits over the horse's head (including the bit and reins), used to guide or control the animal.

**CANTER** - A slow gallop.

**CHARIOT** - A two-wheeled vehicle drawn by horses and driven in a standing position.

**COAT** - The outer layer of hair on a horse.

**DEWORMING** (de-WURM-ing) - To take away worms.

**DOMESTICATED** (doe-MES-tih-kay-ted) - To be of use to and live with man.

**EQUIPMENT** (e-QWIP-ment) - Saddles and bridles.

**GROOM** - To clean.

**HALTER** - A rope or strap used for leading or tying an animal.

**HEADSTALL** - A part of a bridle that encircles the horse's head.

**HERD** - To group animals together.

**HOOF** - A horse's foot.

**LUNGE** - Any sudden forward movement.

**MANE** - The long, heavy hair on the back of a horse's neck.

**MARE** - A female horse over three years old.

**MIDDLE EAST** - A region from the eastern Mediterranean to Iran.

**MUZZLE** - The face of the horse that includes the nose, mouth and jaws.

**NURSE** - To feed a young horse milk from the mother's breast.

**NUTRITION** (noo-TRISH-in) - The use of food for energy.

**PUREBRED** - Unmixed with other breeds.

**REINS** - Narrow straps attached to a bit at either side of the horse's mouth and used to control the horse.

**SADDLE** - A seat for a rider on a horse's back.

**SIRE** - The male parent of a horse.

**STABLE** - Where a horse is housed.

**THOROUGHBRED** - A horse descended from a breed first developed at the end of the eighteenth century by crossing English mares with Arabian stallions.  They are trained for horse racing.

**TRIMMING** - To cut back a horse's hoof.

**TROT** - To run but not fast.

# BIBLIOGRAPHY

Millar, Jane.  *Birth of a Foal.* J. P. Lippincott Company, New York, 1987.

Patent, Dorothy Hinshaw. *A Horse of a Different Color.* Dodd, Mead and Company, New York, 1988.
————.*Horses of America.* Holiday House, New York,1981.

Possell, Elsa.  *Horses.* Childrens Press, Chicago,  1961.

# Index